What Do We Know About
the Kraken?

by Ben Hubbard

illustrated by Robert Squier

Penguin Workshop

For Kimbo, Harv, and Cisco: the Sydney crew—BH

For my brother Mike, who inspired in me a lifelong
enthusiasm for monsters and cryptids—RS

PENGUIN WORKSHOP
An imprint of Penguin Random House LLC, New York

First published in the United States of America by Penguin Workshop,
an imprint of Penguin Random House LLC, New York, 2024

Visit us online at penguinrandomhouse.com.

Library of Congress Cataloging-in-Publication Data is available.

Printed in the United States of America

ISBN 9780593658451 (paperback)   10 9 8 7 6 5 4 3 2 1 WOR
ISBN 9780593658468 (library binding)   10 9 8 7 6 5 4 3 2 1 WOR

Contents

What Do We Know About the Kraken?

One October morning in 1873, two fishermen spotted something strange floating in the cold gray waters of Conception Bay, Newfoundland, Canada. The object looked big, like a lost sail or part of a shipwreck. But as the fishermen rowed their small boat closer, they found it to be something quite different.

It was a mass, dark red in color, and quivering like a giant mound of Jell-O.

One of the fishermen, Theophilus Picot, picked up a long pole and poked at the large heap. Suddenly, it sprang to life. The men had disturbed a huge sea creature and it was now attacking them. The animal rose up from the water and rammed the boat with its sharp beak.

As the men tried to steady themselves, two tentacles (long, thin armlike limbs) shot into the air and then twined around the boat. The tentacles were powerful and covered with round suckers. It was clear that the creature was trying to pull the boat under the water.

Reacting quickly, Picot grabbed a hatchet and began to hack at the tentacles. Although they

were as big around as his arm, Picot completely severed the two tentacles. A thick, black fluid spewed from the creature and darkened the water around the boat. The mysterious animal slid back into the water and began to swim away. After a few moments, it slipped beneath the surface, leaving a black stream behind it. It was not seen again.

The two men returned to port with one of the greatest fishing stories of all time. And to prove what had happened was true, they brought with them a nineteen-foot-long tentacle! Unfortunately, the other captured tentacle had begun to stink so badly that the fishermen had complained and thrown it overboard.

But what kind of creature had the tentacles belonged to? Could this be the same animal that sailors had been describing for thousands of years: a massive, multiarmed monster that lurked deep beneath the surface and rose without warning to take down entire ships and their crews? Had the Newfoundland fishermen just come face-to-face with the legendary creature known as the "Kraken"?

CHAPTER 1
The Ancient Kraken

It seems as if people have been scared of sea monsters since human history began. From the moment we set foot in the water, we could see it was full of strange creatures that we knew nothing about. Man-eating sharks, venomous stingrays, and slithering sea snakes were some of the dangerous animals that sometimes came close to the shore. Fishermen in boats told stories about even larger, lesser-known creatures.

Stingray

In the ancient world, sailors aboard oceangoing ships reported massive beasts seen in the wide-open waters. Some of these were described as large enough to sink large ships.

Thousands of years ago, stories about such creatures were repeated as songs and poems for entertainment. This is known as an oral history. But sea monsters even appeared in one of the world's first written poems, the *Odyssey*, around 700 BCE. The *Odyssey* was composed by Homer. It tells the story of the hero Odysseus (say: O-DIS-e-us) traveling home after the Trojan War. On his ten-year journey, Odysseus sails through a stretch of water guarded by two terrifying sea monsters: Charybdis (say: CUH-rib-dis) and Scylla (say: SIL-uh).

Homer

Unknown Oceans

The world's oceans are a massive, mysterious place. Seawater covers over two-thirds of our planet's surface. It is the largest environment for life on Earth. Yet, around 95 percent of the seas and oceans remain unexplored by humans. To date,

we have found and classified 226,000 species of marine creatures. That's only around 10 percent of the total number! Scientists say there are still millions of species waiting to be discovered. Who knows what creatures are living in the darkest depths of our seas and oceans?

Charybdis

Charybdis is a supernatural monster with flippers, instead of arms and legs, that sinks ships by creating whirlpools. Living opposite Charybdis is the monster Scylla, which is a serpent with six heads, and jaws full of sharklike teeth. Scarier still are Scylla's twelve legs. These are giant tentacles, which it uses to snatch sailors off their ships to devour them. According to ancient Greek mythology, the sea god Poseidon controlled

Charybdis and Scylla, and unleashed them on Odysseus as he sailed past.

The *Odyssey* is an ancient poem about mythical heroes and monsters. But several centuries later, sea creatures that resembled Scylla began appearing in texts written by scholars and historians. Pliny the Elder was one such historian, from ancient Rome.

In around 60 CE, Pliny wrote a book filled with facts about the natural world titled *Naturalis historia.* In this, Pliny described a sea creature he referred to as a "polyp," with a head as big as a barrel

Pliny the Elder

and tentacles thirty feet long. Pliny wrote that polyps have "suckers spread over their arms" and "pour out a dark fluid which these animals have instead of blood, so darkening the water and concealing themselves." Pliny said the polyps swam by shooting water through a tube in their back. They also had a terrible smell. Pliny wrote that polyps could be dangerous. He

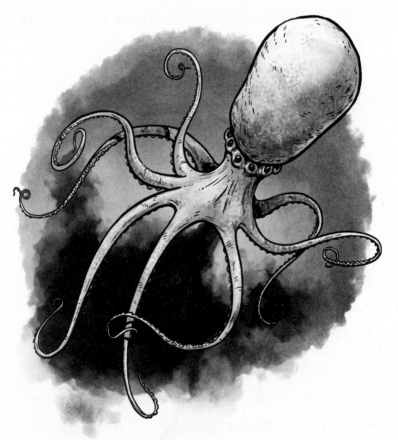

Polyp

said that when a polyp attacks a person "it struggles with him by coiling around him and swallows him with sucker-cups and drags him asunder." Pliny used the word "asunder" to mean "into pieces."

Pliny was not the last person to describe such a creature. Stories about similar animals continued through the ages. They are even told today. The animals in these stories share many characteristics. They have long, thick, sucker-covered tentacles or arms; a terrible smell, often like urine; large eyes, sometimes as big as dinner plates; and aggressive and destructive personalities.

The last point is perhaps the most important. In the centuries after Pliny, sailors reported a giant monster rising up from the deep to attack their ships. Sometimes the monster would wrap its tentacles around the masts to sink the vessel. The creature was big—some said it was the size of an island.

No one knew exactly what this monster was, but many tried to find out. However, it would be

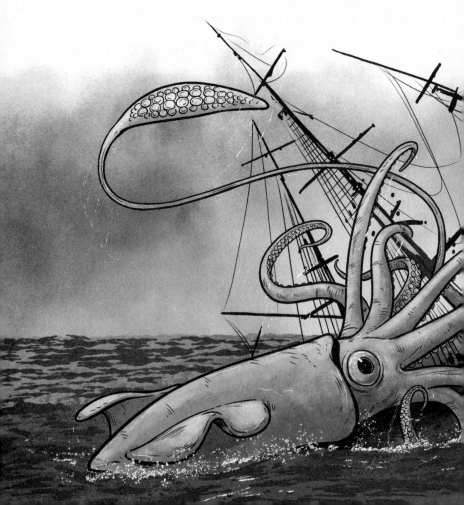

many centuries after Homer's Scylla and Pliny's polyp that the creature was given its modern name. It was a name that struck terror in the hearts of sailors and fishermen who heard it: Kraken.

Greek Mythological Monsters

Many famous sea monsters appeared in stories from Greek mythology. These myths were usually about gods, goddesses, and heroes, and at one time were considered to be true. In one such Greek myth, the hero Perseus battles the sea monster Cetus. He turns Cetus to stone using the head of another monster, Medusa.

In another myth, the hero Hercules slays a nine-headed sea monster called the Lernaean (say: ler-NEE-an) Hydra. This was difficult because if one of the Hydra's heads was removed, two more would grow back in its place. Circe was another sea creature who was also a goddess. She could turn humans into animals.

Medusa

CHAPTER 2
Scandinavian Sightings

For hundreds of years after Pliny, there were few written reports about a tentacled sea monster. When it next appeared, it was far away from the warm Mediterranean waters of ancient Greece and Rome. Instead, the new sightings emerged around the icy waters of Scandinavia, an area that now includes the countries of Norway, Sweden, and Denmark.

Some of these sightings were recorded by Swedish historian Olaus Magnus in his 1555 history book, *A Description of the Northern Peoples*. In the book, Magnus described a creature that was a cross between a fish and a squid. It had huge eyes and "hairs like goose feathers, thick and long, like a beard hanging down." It could easily drown sailors and sink ships, Magnus wrote.

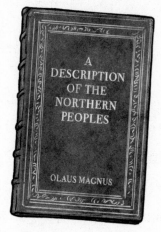

Magnus included illustrations of this sea monster in his book. And because he was a respected scholar, the illustrations were copied and published in history books in other countries. This convinced people of the time that massive sea monsters were simply a fact of life. Sailors were not surprised. Some said they had seen such monsters during their time at sea.

But sailors were not the only people reporting strange sightings. In 1734, a Danish Norwegian missionary named Hans Egede saw a giant serpent-like creature. He said it had pulled up alongside his ship, near the coast of Greenland. According to Egede, the animal's body was four times longer than the ship and its head higher than its mast! The creature did not attack Egede's ship, but instead dived away beneath the waves.

Hans Egede

Back on land, Egede discussed what he had seen with several Norwegian fishermen. They told him the creature was the monster they called Hafgufa.

The missionary wrote about the creature in his book, *A Description of Greenland*: "A great ghastly sea monster now and then appears in the main sea, which they call Kracken, and is no doubt the same that the islanders call Hafgufa."

Hafgufa

The Hafgufa is a giant sea monster from Viking mythology. It is mentioned in the Viking stories known as the *Sagas*. The *Sagas* were written in the thirteenth century by Icelandic author Snorri Sturluson.

In the *Sagas*, the Hafgufa is described as a large, dark mass floating just below the surface. When it stays still, it can be mistaken for an island. At other times, it drifts beneath boats and has a putrid smell like "a hundred wet dogs." Some said the Hafgufa was the same creature as the Kraken. Others thought it was more likely to be a type of large whale.

Egede's description is interesting because it is one of the first times that the word Kracken (later changed to Kraken) appears in a book. Kraken comes from the Norwegian word *krake*, which originally meant "pole" or "uprooted tree." Over time, however, the word *krake* came to mean "fabulous sea monster."

This is how Swedish scientist Carolus Linnaeus used the word in his famous 1735 book, *Systema Naturae*, which described a system of classifying the natural world. Later, Linnaeus identified the Kraken as "a unique monster" living in the seas of Norway. He also classified the Kraken as a cephalopod.

Carolus Linnaeus

Cephalopods are the animals that include squid, octopuses, and cuttlefish. They are easy to recognize because they have multiple arms or tentacles. However, Linnaeus wrote that he had never actually seen a Kraken himself. This made it hard to believe he could classify it as a cephalopod or "a unique monster." Perhaps Linnaeus also realized this, as the Kraken was removed from later editions of *Systema Naturae*.

But in 1735, when the book was first published, many people began to believe that the Kraken was real and probably a cephalopod. A giant octopus or squid seemed most likely.

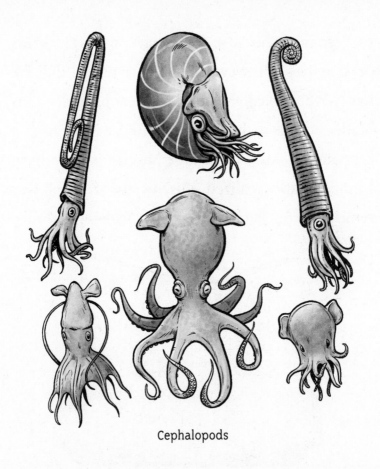

Cephalopods

Around this same time, another Scandinavian made it his business to learn more about the Kraken. Erik Pontoppidan was a Danish bishop writing a book titled *The Natural History of Norway*. He was fascinated by the Kraken and wanted to include it in his book. To research the Kraken, Pontoppidan interviewed Norwegian fishermen and sailors who claimed to have seen it.

The fishermen's and sailors' descriptions of the Kraken were similar to those told to Hans Egede some years earlier. And although he was writing a history book, Pontoppidan repeated the descriptions as facts without questioning them. When Pontoppidan's book was published in 1752, it said that the Kraken "seems to be about an English mile and a half in circumference (some would say more)."

Pontoppidan was just repeating what he had been told, but his calculations of the Kraken's size were too big to be believed.

Bishop Pontoppidan

By the early 1700s, people had made great voyages of discovery around the entire world. Many extraordinary creatures had been found. But no one had ever found a sea monster a "mile and a half in circumference." Many people were unconvinced by Pontoppidan's account and some were very critical of it.

However, some aspects of Pontoppidan's Kraken were more believable. He noted that the Kraken had a "strong and peculiar scent" and spewed out a black liquid which "appears quite thick and turbid." If those criticizing Pontoppidan had paused for a moment, they might have realized that the bishop was describing a type of cephalopod, such as a squid, or octopus.

Even though people doubted Pontoppidan, they continued to believe in the creature known as the Kraken. And in the next century, new reports about the creature would help cement its place as a ship-attacking monster.

A squid inking

CHAPTER 3
The Disgrace of de Montfort

In the nineteenth century, stories about the Kraken continued. Sightings of long-armed monsters were reported in newspapers, magazines, and books. But no one yet had definitively established what kind of creature the Kraken might be. One scientist, however, was sure he had the answer. Pierre Denys de Montfort was a French scientist who studied mollusks—the group of creatures without backbones that includes cephalopods. Snails, slugs, and clams are mollusks, and so are squid and octopuses. Octopuses also happened to be de Montfort's specialty.

Pierre Denys de Montfort

De Montfort had become fascinated with octopuses in 1783 after talking to a whaling ship captain. At the time, the ship had been hunting sperm whales—the largest toothed predator in the world. After one whale had been caught, the captain saw something sticking out of its mouth.

The object was "the arm of an enormous octopus whose sunken suckers were broader as that of a hat," the captain said. These suckers were arranged in rows on the arm, just like a common octopus. The whole arm was around forty-two feet long and was probably bitten off during a great battle.

It was an incredible story, which de Montfort absolutely loved. He was convinced that the Kraken was real and also sure that it was an octopus. He decided to write a book about the subject, *A General and Particular Natural History of Mollusks*, which he published in 1802. To research the book, de Montfort talked to many sailors and fishermen with stories about the Kraken. Like Bishop Pontoppidan before him, de Montfort believed all of the stories and repeated them in his book as facts.

One story was about a giant octopus that had attacked a ship off the coast of Angola, Africa. The octopus was reported to have arms as tall as the masts, which it wrapped around the ship, trying to sink it. The sailors on board grabbed axes and swords and slashed at the arms until the creature let go. The sailors felt lucky to have survived the encounter.

When de Montfort repeated this story in his book, he included an illustration to go with it. The drawing was of a giant octopus, with its arms wrapped around the masts of a ship.

It shocked and fascinated readers everywhere. Because de Montfort was a mollusk expert, people accepted the picture in his book as factually correct. It helped confirm the legend of the Kraken as a sea monster and a giant octopus. It also inspired writers such as poet Alfred Tennyson to write about the Kraken.

As de Montfort's fame grew, so did his stories

about giant octopus attacks on ships. In one story, de Montfort said that he had heard that a giant octopus had attacked English and French warships during a sea battle. The octopus had sunk four British and six French ships. It was an extraordinary story. It was also untrue. In actual fact, the ships in the story had not been sunk, but were floating safely in the Caribbean Sea. None of the ships' captains had reported seeing a giant octopus, let alone been attacked by one.

Tennyson's Kraken

Alfred, Lord Tennyson

Alfred, Lord Tennyson, was an English poet (1809–1892) who created now-famous phrases such as "'Tis better to have loved and lost than never to have loved at all" and "A lie that is half-truth is the darkest of all lies."

In 1830, Tennyson wrote a poem titled "The Kraken," which begins:

Below the thunders of the upper deep,

Far, far beneath in the abysmal sea,

His ancient, dreamless, uninvaded sleep

The Kraken sleepeth.

By this time, the Kraken had moved beyond the world of sailors and scientists and was now being talked about by authors and poets.

This scandal ruined the scientist's reputation. De Montfort claimed he was only joking, but he was no longer believed to be trustworthy. He moved to the French countryside to become a beekeeper. Some reports say he died of starvation in around 1820.

But by then, de Montfort's book and its illustration had convinced many people that the Kraken was a giant octopus. Perhaps this was not surprising. The sightings throughout the centuries had reported an oversize creature that looked like an octopus. So, was it possible? Was de Montfort correct in thinking the Kraken was a type of giant octopus?

Without a time machine that doubles as a deep-sea submarine, we will never know for sure. But scientists know a lot more about octopuses now than they did in the 1800s. And experts say that an octopus large enough to rise out of the water and attack a ship is unlikely.

Today, the largest known octopus in the world is the giant Pacific octopus. It is a deep-sea dweller that typically grows to around sixteen feet long and weighs around one hundred ten pounds. The largest giant Pacific octopus ever seen was observed in the water off Port Hardy in British Columbia, Canada. It was estimated to be thirty feet long and weigh around six hundred pounds—although it was not actually caught or measured accurately. However, even this octopus would have little success in trying to pull an entire ship beneath the water's surface.

Giant Pacific octopus

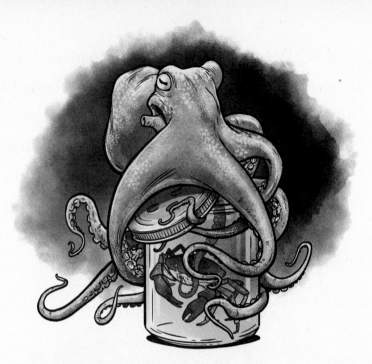

Would an octopus actually want or need to sink a ship? Octopuses are supersmart. They can navigate through mazes, solve puzzles for fun, and learn to unscrew jars to get the food inside. Octopuses being studied at New Zealand's University of Otago even figured out how to turn off the laboratory lights from their aquariums. They did this by squirting jets of water at the light switch.

Octopuses also have an amazing sense of touch. Their arms are filled with the same sensors and neurons found in their brains. This means that an octopus's arm can smell, taste, and touch all by itself. If an octopus's arm is removed from its body, it will keep performing the same task for a while independently. So would a giant Pacific octopus attack a ship by accident, thinking it was food or that there was food on board? It does not make sense: People and ships are not on the octopus's menu. Instead, they eat fish, squid, crabs, shrimp, and, very occasionally, seabirds.

The theory that the Kraken was an octopus, therefore, did not seem to fit. So, if the Kraken wasn't an octopus, what was it? The main clue may be found in the suckered arms or tentacles often described in sailors' stories about the Kraken.

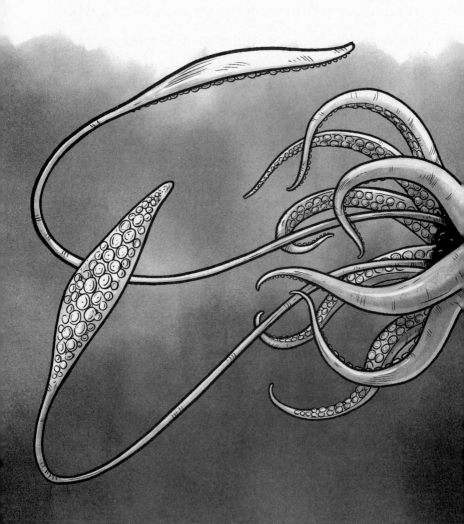

In his description of a polyp, Pliny said it attacked a person by "coiling round him and it swallows him with sucker-cups and drags him asunder." What, then, if the sucker cups belonged not to an octopus's arms but a squid's?

Squid

Moby Dick

American author Herman Melville's 1851 novel *Moby-Dick* is about the quest for a giant white whale. But the book also  contains a scene with a squid-like creature. One of the characters in the book calls it: "The great live squid, which, they say, few whale-ships ever beheld, and returned to their ports to tell of it." The book goes on to describe the squid as "a vast pulpy mass, furlongs in length and breadth, of a glancing cream-color, lay floating on the water, innumerable long arms radiating from its centre, and curling and twisting like a nest of anacondas, as if blindly to clutch at any hapless object in reach."

Herman Melville

Interestingly, Melville mentions the work of Bishop Pontoppidan in *Moby-Dick*. He writes: "There seems some ground to imagine that the great Kraken of Bishop Pontoppidan may ultimately resolve itself into Squid." What the author means by this is that the Kraken may one day turn out to be a giant squid.

The squid theory seemed to fit. And from the mid-nineteenth century, several reports also appeared to confirm it. In 1856, along the New England coast of the United States, a whaler named Charles Nordhoff wrote that sperm whales fed on creatures "known among whalemen as 'squid.'" He wrote that these squid were believed by whalers to be "much larger than the largest whale, even exceeding in size the hull of a large vessel." Other whalers said sperm whales would often spew up massive pieces of squid as they died.

Charles Nordhoff

Authors who wrote fiction also seemed to become more drawn to the idea of the Kraken as a squid rather than an octopus. In his *Twenty Thousand Leagues Under the Sea*, science fiction author Jules Verne wrote about exactly such a creature. In the book,  the submarine *Nautilus* is attacked by a school of massive squid the characters call "devilfish" and "poulps." They even mention Kraken researchers Olaus Magnus and Bishop Pontoppidan while discussing the creatures.

In Verne's book, there is an illustration that is clearly based on de Montfort's octopus illustration. However, some important details have been changed. The illustration shows a creature with a large tail, round eyes, and a longer body. It is clearly more of a squid than an octopus.

So, if the Kraken was indeed a type of squid, where was the proof? Without evidence, how could anyone be sure that a squid large enough to be the legendary Kraken could exist?

Jules Verne (1828–1905)

Born in 1828, Jules Verne was a best-selling French author who is often remembered as the "Father of science fiction." His books about voyages aboard fantastic machines through space, sea, and time include *Journey to the Center of the Earth*, *Twenty Thousand Leagues Under the Sea*, and *Around the World in Eighty Days*.

Verne had also worked as a lawyer and stockbroker before quitting to write novels, plays, and poems full-time. Today, Jules Verne is the second most translated author in the world, after English crime novelist Agatha Christie.

CHAPTER 4
Serpents and Scientific Discovery

In 1861, an exciting encounter took place in the Canary Islands, off the coast of West Africa. Here, the French warship *Alecton* saw a large animal floating on the water's surface. Captain Frederic Bouyer said the creature was brick red, around eighteen feet long, and had glimmering green eyes that frightened the crew.

The creature did not stir when the ship drew closer, and Bouyer decided to try to capture it. The crew fired rifles at the

Alecton

animal and threw ropes around it to haul it on
board. As they managed to lasso it, the creature
discharged a dark liquid and let off a strong musky

smell. Unfortunately, the rope cut through the animal's body and only the tail was brought on board.

Bouyer's report on the creature was sent to the French Academy of Sciences. His description of the creature's mouth was of particular interest. Since the mid-1850s, serious scientists had taken an active interest in the giant squid

many supposed was the Kraken. Bouyer wrote that "Its mouth like the beak of a parakeet, could open nearly a half meter" (about a foot and a half). The idea that the Kraken could have a beak was a surprise to many

Close-up view of squid beak

scientists—but not to Danish biology professor Japetus Steenstrup.

Steenstrup actually had such a beak in his possession! The rare beak had been taken from a large sea creature that had washed up on a

Danish shore. It was the size of a grapefruit, and Steenstrup kept it in a jar to show other scientists. It was similar to beaks found on smaller squid, but it was much bigger.

Japetus Steenstrup

Like previous Kraken researchers, such as Olaus Magnus, Hans Egede, Bishop Pontoppidan, and Denys de Montfort, Steenstrup had become fascinated by the Kraken after reading eyewitness accounts about the creature. But Steenstrup was not satisfied simply with sailors' stories. He wanted actual evidence that the Kraken existed.

Luckily, he had the first piece of evidence: the beak. Steenstrup believed that it belonged to a rarely seen sea creature he named *Architeuthis dux*, which became known as the "giant squid."

The giant squid would fit most of the descriptions of the Kraken: long tentacles, large eyes, a bad smell, and capable of discharging a dark liquid. However, unless Steenstrup could provide an actual specimen of this giant squid, it would be impossible to convince other scientists it existed.

Then, in the 1870s, something incredible happened. As if on cue, giant squid began washing up on seashores, mainly along the eastern coast of Canada. In 1871, a fishing boat found a partly eaten giant squid on a shore in Newfoundland. Its tentacles were around fifteen feet long. The fishermen took a photo and sent it to Japetus Steenstrup, who now had photographic proof that the giant squid existed.

Then, in 1873, came the attack on the two fishermen in Newfoundland's Conception Bay. During the attack, the squid wrapped its tentacles around the boat and tried to sink it.

The fishermen had cut off the two tentacles. The men did not know about Japetus Steenstrup, but they were friends with Moses Harvey, a local reverend and naturalist. They took one of the tentacles to show him.

Moses Harvey

Harvey was a well-known journalist who had published articles in newspapers across North America and Britain. Harvey's favorite subject was sea monsters, and he immediately identified the squid tentacle as "the veritable arm of the hitherto mythical devilfish." Harvey then wrote an article about the fishermen's encounter for a magazine, the *Maritime Monthly*.

Soon after the article was published, a whole squid body was found and taken to Moses Harvey's home. The squid was enormous—more than thirty feet long! Harvey hung it over a bathtub and photographed it. Harvey's article, the attack on the fishermen, and now a massive squid specimen were enough to convince many people that the mystery of the Kraken had been solved. Simply, the Kraken of myth and legend was actually the giant squid—and there was not just one of them, but many.

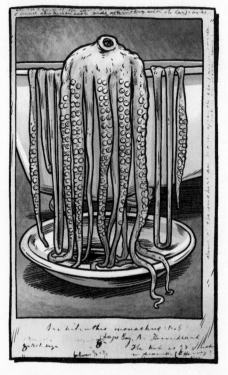

However, if this theory was true, why had the Kraken decided to show itself now and in such large numbers? No one could be sure.

Giant Squid vs. Sperm Whale

On July 8, 1875, the crew aboard the US ship *Pauline* reported seeing a battle between a sperm whale and a "sea serpent." As reported in the newspaper *The Illustrated London News*, Captain

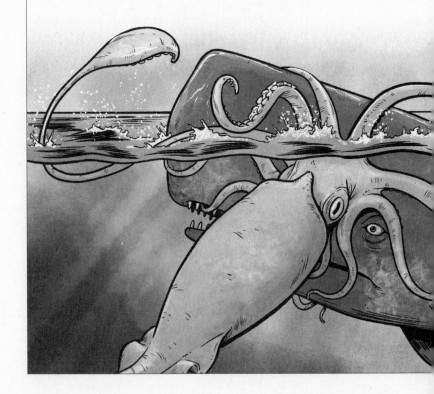

George Drevar said the incident occurred while he was sailing off the coast of Brazil. This is where the *Pauline* came across a "monstrous sea-serpent coiled twice round a large sperm-whale." Drevar said the serpent then pulled the whale below the surface, where "no doubt it was gorged at the serpent's leisure."

Moses Harvey began sending some of the squid pieces he had collected to an American expert. Addison Verrill was professor of zoology at Connecticut's Yale University and a squid specialist. Verrill had been collecting and cataloging specimens of the giant squid that had washed up throughout the 1870s. Through this work, Verrill was able to build a giant squid model for display in the Yale Peabody Museum. Verrill believed it was a scientist's job to explain their research to the world. He therefore gave public lectures on the giant squid and was the subject of an 1880 *New York Times* article "Monsters of the Ocean."

Addison Verrill

By the late 1880s, however, parts of the giant squid stopped washing up on seashores. It was as if the squid had appeared to prove they did indeed exist, and then, after much publicity, retired back to their lives of deep-sea solitude. To many people, it seemed like the riddle of the Kraken had been solved. The Kraken and the giant squid were simply the same thing.

But not everybody was convinced. For Kraken researchers and squid scientists, some things did not add up. In reality, a giant squid big enough to sink a ship had never been found. Scientists could therefore not be sure they grew to such sizes. Could anyone be certain that the giant squid really was the creature known as the Kraken?

CHAPTER 5
What's in a Giant Squid?

The washed-up giant squid of the 1870s had been a great gift for scientists—literally. Now they had specimen jars filled with preserving chemicals and giant-squid body parts. They could study the giant squid in depth. What they found surprised them. The giant squid was a creature unlike anything they had ever seen. It was something of a biological wonder. So what, then, makes the giant squid so amazing?

One of the most remarkable parts of the giant squid are its arms and tentacles. Situated at the front of its body, a giant squid has eight arms and two tentacles. The tentacles are long, thick, and stretchy, like they are made from rubber or elastic. Sometimes this can make their true length difficult to calculate. However, the longest giant squid tentacles found were twenty-six feet in length. That's about as long as a school bus.

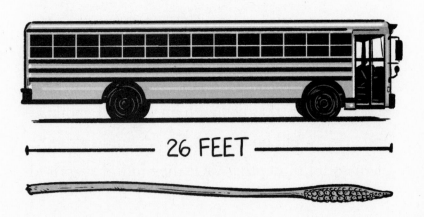

26 FEET

The tentacles are a little longer than the arms because they are used to grab prey, the animals the squid hunts for food. A giant squid's prey is almost any creature that comes close, including fish, shrimp, and other squid. When it spies its prey, the squid's tentacles shoot out and grab it. The tentacles have clubs at the end, which look like oven mitts. They lock together like hands to keep prey trapped and draw it in.

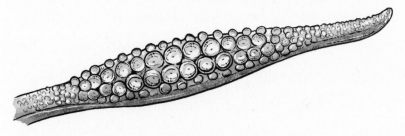

Close-up view of a giant squid's club

As the tentacles pull the squid's meal toward its mouth, its eight arms wrap around it. There is little any prey can do to save itself at that point. That's because it is being tightly gripped by rows of suckers along the squid's arms and tentacles.

Close-up view of a giant
squid's suckers

The giant squid's suckers are not soft like an octopus's. Instead, each sucker has a round ring of teeth inside it. This ring looks a bit like a cookie cutter for making round shapes in dough. As the sucker squishes onto a prey's skin to hold it tight, the teeth cut into the prey's flesh to make sure it can't move. Now that the smaller animal is in a viselike grip, the arms pull it to the squid's open beak.

The beak is situated at the bottom of the squid's head. It is made from a hard, sharp substance called chitin. This can easily slice through flesh and cut it into bite-size pieces. Inside the beak is a tonguelike muscle covered with tiny blades, also made from chitin. Called a radula, it is like a cheese-grating tongue that shreds the flesh of its prey.

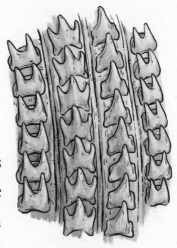

Radula

Above the beak, on either side of the squid's head, are its eyes. These can grow to a foot in diameter and are some of the largest eyes in the animal kingdom. Inside the head is the squid's small, donut-shaped brain. This helps it detect prey and evade predators, any animal that could kill and eat it.

Below the squid's head is an oar-shaped body part called a mantle. It is often mistaken for the squid's head, but the mantle is actually the squid's tail. It has fins on either side to help the squid steer. The mantle is where all of the squid's organs can be found, such as its liver and heart. On the underside of the mantle is a funnel. To move, a squid sucks in water to fill up the mantle like a balloon. It then squirts out a jet of water through the funnel, which pushes it in the opposite direction. This is a form of movement known as jet propulsion.

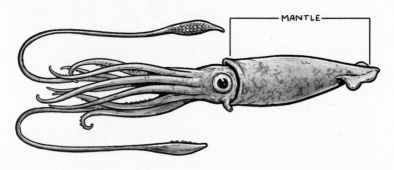

MANTLE

But movement is not all the squid uses its funnel for. The funnel is also used to lay eggs, expel waste, and squirt out black ink. By squirting out this ink, a squid clouds the water around it. This confuses approaching predators and provides cover so the squid can make a quick getaway.

The giant squid has a wide hunting range.

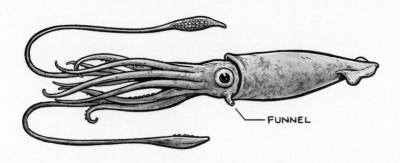

FUNNEL

It can travel along the surface of the sea and then quickly descend several feet. To do this, it produces and expels the chemical ammonia—a foul-smelling waste product found in urine. It is also very light. By filling its body with ammonia, a giant squid is light enough to rise upward to the water's surface. By then expelling the ammonia through its funnel, the squid can descend downward. Ammonia, therefore, accounts for the very bad smell reported by sailors during giant-squid encounters. It also means the giant squid cannot be eaten by humans, unlike other species of squid. This is because its high level of ammonia makes it poisonous to humans.

Apart from hunting, the giant squid is

primarily a creature of the deep ocean. It mainly lives between 1,650 and 3,300 feet below the surface. At this depth, the pressure from all the water above would be too much for a person to survive outside a submarine. They would simply be crushed. The deep sea is also icy cold. This is the domain of fascinating fish that make their

own light, and large predators, such as the giant squid.

The giant squid is one of the ocean's largest predators. But it is hunted by an even bigger creature: the sperm whale. The remains of giant squid are often found in the stomachs of sperm whales. It is thought that the whales eat hundreds, if not thousands, of giant squid every year. This is no easy task: To catch a squid, a whale must hold its breath, dive hundreds of feet, then find the squid in near-total darkness. The whale does this by sending out a clicking sound from its uniquely shaped snout. The sound bounces off objects and returns to the whale. This method of hunting and navigating, called echolocation (say: EK-oh-loh-KAY-shun), is also used by bats on land.

A sperm whale locked in a battle with a giant squid could explain some of the Kraken sightings at sea. As well as finding giant squid pieces in sperm whale stomachs, fishermen have also found round cookie-cutter wounds on the whales. This is clear evidence of the whale being caught in— and marked by—a giant squid's suckers.

For nineteenth-century scientists, the giant squid theory seemed to fit with the Kraken sightings throughout the centuries. But the size of the Kraken in these sightings could not be explained. There was nothing to show that a giant squid could reach the sizes described by sailors and fishermen. The scientists thought this could be explained as tall tales told by people who had been at sea too long. After all, even some of the best fishermen sometimes exaggerate about the "one that got away."

But then, near the dawn of the twentieth century, something strange happened. Sperm whales were discovered with different-looking scars. These had the same round cookie-cutter teeth marks as before, but inside these rings were a kind of sharp, hook-like wound. These marks could not have been made by the giant squid.

Was it possible there was an even bigger squid than the giant squid? The largest known giant squid measured forty-three feet long, although scientists believed they could reach up to sixty-six feet. Experts did not think there could be a larger squid than that. But it would not be long before something happened to change their minds.

CHAPTER 6
Giant and Colossal

In 1909, off the coast of Massachusetts, sailors aboard the *Annie Perry* fishing boat saw a giant squid in the water. They tried to haul it on board but were unable to grab it without pulling it into pieces. A seven-foot-long tentacle did survive, however. This began a new era of giant-squid sightings.

And this was not the only squid making the news. In 1925, squid arms and tentacles were found in a sperm whale's stomach in Antarctica, which changed everything. The arms looked like they belonged to a giant squid, but they were longer and thicker than anything seen before. They were also armed with a terrifying weapon. Each arm was covered with the same cookie-cutter suckers as the giant squid, but in the center of each sucker was a curved hook, like the claw of a tiger. On the end of the tentacles, the hooks could also swivel around, making it a lethal tool to dig deep into the flesh of other animals.

A British zoologist named Guy Robson studied the arms and tentacles and said they belonged to a new, never-before-seen creature. He named it *Mesonychoteuthis hamiltoni*, because *Mesonychoteuthis* means "middle claw," and a man named E. Hamilton was the sailor who discovered the remains. The creature became commonly known as the colossal squid. Some scientists thought it might be possible for the squid to grow to one hundred fifty feet long. However, decades passed and no more colossal squid arms and tentacles were found.

Guy Robson

Was the colossal creature a singular mutant giant squid? Had the sea monster known as the Kraken finally revealed itself, only to be lost forever or devoured by a sperm whale?

Frederick Aldrich

While scientists pondered these questions, something exciting happened in the world of the giant squid. In the 1950s, a marine biologist named Frederick Aldrich had been studying the unexplained strandings of the giant squid in the 1870s. He believed cold water currents had pushed the squid out of their deep-sea habitat and into shallower waters and shores. He also suggested the same currents could occur every ninety years. Then, almost like clockwork, this exact thing happened. In the 1960s, giant squid began appearing in great numbers. However, this time they were not only appearing in the waters off the coast of Eastern Canada but much farther south.

After being proven right about the timing of the currents, Aldrich became one of the top giant-squid hunters in the world. He even put up signs along the coast of Canada's Newfoundland that read: "Wanted! Dead or Alive: . . . giant squid."

Two fishermen did find a whole dead giant squid floating in a Newfoundland bay and sent it to Aldrich. It weighed 331 pounds and was thirty feet long.

It then became Aldrich's mission to achieve what no scientist had before and observe a giant squid in the wild. But finding the creature proved to be an impossible task.

USS *Stein*

In 1978, a warship called the USS *Stein* hit something large in the North Atlantic Ocean.

After investigating, the crew reported the ship's SONAR had been damaged. (SONAR uses sound waves to detect objects below the water.) Once the ship was back at the dock, strange round cuts were found all over the ship's steel and rubber SONAR dome. The circular cuts also showed evidence of a sharp, hooked claw. Experts later realized that this type of damage must have been made by a colossal squid.

Then in 1981, a new discovery once again rocked the world of squid scientists and Kraken researchers. While fishing in the waters around Antarctica, a Russian fishing trawler caught a colossal squid! The fishermen pulled the creature onto the deck, then photographed and measured it. It was thirteen feet long and clearly not yet fully grown. Unfortunately, the fishermen threw the colossal squid back into the water as they had no way to preserve it and keep it from rotting.

In 2003, there was even more sensational news: A colossal squid had been caught off the coast of Antarctica. The squid died, but its body was sent to a laboratory in nearby New Zealand. And in 2005 and 2007, two more colossal squid bodies were found around Antarctica and also sent to New Zealand. The 2007 body was kept on ice in New Zealand for more than a year while scientists figured out how to dissect it (carefully cut apart the animal's insides to study it).

In New Zealand in 2008, biologists Steve O'Shea, Tsunemi Kubodera, and Kat Bolstad thawed out the colossal squid to dissect it. The first thing the scientists noticed was that the squid had shrunk during the freezing process. It was now only thirteen feet long, but had originally been twenty-six feet. The most amazing feature of this squid was its eyes: They measured eleven inches across, making them the largest animal eyes yet discovered.

Caught on Camera

Tsunemi Kubodera

It was Frederick Aldrich's dream to see a live giant squid. However, he did not achieve this during his lifetime. But in 2004, a Japanese biologist named Tsunemi Kubodera succeeded where Aldrich had failed. While on his research ship in the Pacific Ocean's Ogasawara Islands,

Kubodera photographed a giant squid caught on a fishing line.

Then, in 2006, Kubodera topped his own achievement. This time, a giant squid grabbed some bait at the end of Kubodera's fishing line and wouldn't let go. The huge, dark-red squid struggled with the line as the crew tried to bring it on board. It was the first time a giant squid had been filmed and was a major milestone for giant-squid research. Sadly, the squid did not survive the encounter.

Te Papa

Because colossal squid were found in Antarctic waters, they were taken to biologists who specialize in squid in nearby New Zealand. The biologists were then able to examine the squid at the Museum of New Zealand Te Papa Tongarewa.

Te Papa Tongarewa roughly translates to "container of treasures" in Maori, the language of the indigenous people of New Zealand. After the squid biologists researched the squid found in Antarctica, they were put on display at Te Papa. The museum now has three colossal squid exhibitions, including the only complete colossal squid specimen in the world.

The squid's beak, too, was large: over an inch and a half. Because larger colossal squid beaks have been found in the stomachs of sperm whales, scientists realized the specimen was probably a baby. A fully grown colossal squid must therefore be somewhere down in the deep, staying well-hidden. Perhaps the real Kraken will one day reveal itself to the world?

CHAPTER 7
The Popular Kraken

For thousands of years, stories of the Kraken have frightened and fascinated us. Our earliest ancestors were scared of the world below the waves and the creatures within it. No one knew what dwelled there. But over time, tales of a ship-destroying monster became legend. Homer wrote about such a creature in one of the first written poems. By the Middle Ages, the creature had a name: Kraken. And from then on, Kraken researchers searched far and wide to find one. Every now and then, a half-eaten Kraken-like creature would wash up on a beach, or pieces would be discovered in a whale's stomach. For many people, seeing an actual Kraken became an obsession.

Today, this dream is perhaps only a plane ride away. In New Zealand, the colossal squid remains on permanent display. There have also been giant squid exhibitions at the American Museum of Natural History in New York and the Natural History Museum in London. Here, in glass cases

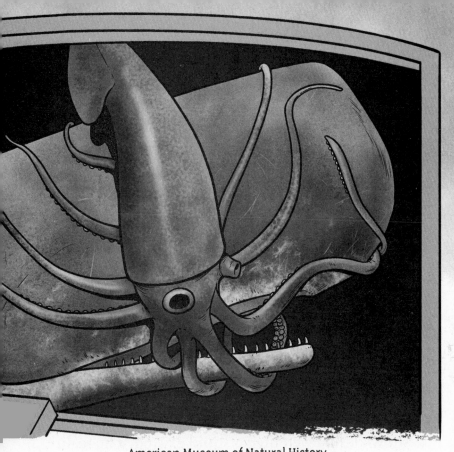

American Museum of Natural History

filled with chemicals to preserve their bodies, the squid reveal their secrets to every visitor. These museum visitors may be staring at a real-life Kraken. Because all current evidence suggests that the colossal squid and the giant squid will most likely be proven to be the same creatures as the Kraken: large eyes, dangerous sucking arms and tentacles, squid ink as a defense, and a terrible ammonia smell. These are the physical characteristics that have been described over the centuries by the sailors, fishermen, and other seagoers who have reported encounters with the Kraken. Both squid have also been shown to attack boats and larger ships.

But in the vast unknown of the world's oceans, nothing can be certain. Many scientists doubted the idea of a forty-three-foot squid, until one was found. Then, the discovery of the colossal squid showed that even bigger squid existed. The reality is that we are still not aware of all the creatures that live in the deep.

Millions of years ago, massive marine reptiles called ichthyosaurs (say: IK-thee-uh-sorz) ruled the seas. They could grow to eighty-five feet long and had enormous snouts, jaws, and teeth.

Benchley's Beast

Peter Benchley was the author of the best-selling 1974 novel *Jaws*. Featuring a man-eating great white shark, the novel was made into a blockbuster movie in 1975 by Steven Spielberg.

In 1991, Benchley published another novel, *Beast*. This book featured a terrifying giant squid, and its cover showed the frightening suckers on its huge tentacle. The squid terrorizes a small seaside town by eating swimmers and sailors. A hunt is then  mounted to kill the squid. But in the end, it is a massive sperm whale that kills it.

Later, giant shark-type creatures named megalodons grew up to fifty-five feet long and had powerful jaws with seven-inch-long teeth. These creatures died out in massive worldwide extinctions.

However, some sea creatures survived these extinctions. In 1938, an ancient fish that was thought to be extinct, called a coelacanth (say: SEE-luh-kanth), was discovered off the coast of South Africa. This means coelacanths have lived in the seas for more than 410 million years! Coelacanths are not large sea monsters, but it proves creatures can outlive mass extinctions. Who knows what ancient creatures therefore remain hidden and undiscovered? Perhaps the Kraken is not the colossal or giant squid but an even older, larger creature waiting to reveal itself.

For now, the possibility of such a creature lives on in books, comics, video games, and film.

The coelacanth that was discovered in 1938

The Kraken is also shown on bottles of deodorant, stamps, and even has its own roller coaster at SeaWorld in Orlando, Florida. Most people are very familiar with the image of the Kraken. The idea of a Kraken is as terrifying and interesting today as it was for our ancestors thousands of years ago. When we see a picture of this sea monster, it is easy to recognize the thick, long tentacles and giant eyes as the massive, aggressive

creature that rises up and attacks from the sea. It is hard, then, not to remember it by name: Kraken.

Kraken roller coaster in Orlando, Florida

Release the Kraken

The Kraken is one of the monsters that star in the 2010 action movie *Clash of the Titans*. A remake of a 1981 movie, *Clash of the Titans* is a story about the exploits of the mythological Greek hero Perseus. In the film, Perseus is tasked with slaying

the Kraken, a terrible monster controlled by the king of the gods, Zeus. It is Zeus who delivers the film's most famous line to begin the battle between man and beast: "Release the Kraken!" The line became an internet meme and popular catchphrase, especially among fans of the NHL team the Seattle Kraken.

Timeline of the Kraken

c. 700 BCE	Ancient Greek poet Homer describes sea monsters Charybdis and Scylla in the *Odyssey*
c. 60 CE	Ancient Roman historian Pliny the Elder writes about a Kraken-type creature he calls a "polyp"
1555	Swedish historian Olaus Magnus describes a sea creature that drowns sailors and sinks ships
1734	Danish Norwegian missionary Hans Egede reports seeing a giant serpent-like creature alongside his ship near Greenland
1735	Swedish scientist Carolus Linnaeus identifies the Kraken as a cephalopod living in the sea near Norway
1802	French scientist Pierre Denys de Montfort describes the Kraken as a type of large octopus
1873	A giant squid attacks a fishing boat in Conception Bay, Newfoundland, Canada
1960	Giant squid begin appearing around the world, particularly in the waters around Antarctica
2004	Japanese biologist Tsunemi Kubodera takes the first photographs of a live giant squid
2008	Biologists Steve O'Shea, Tsunemi Kubodera, and Kat Bolstad dissect a colossal squid for the first time
2010	*Clash of the Titans* film is released, makes "Release the Kraken" an instantly recognizable internet meme

Timeline of the World

700 BCE	Athlete Atheradas of Laconia wins the two-hundred-yard sprint, the stadion race, at the twentieth Olympic Games
60 CE	Boudica, queen of the Iceni tribe, leads a rebellion against the Roman rule of Britain
1555	Humayun, the Mughal ruler of India, takes the throne in Delhi for the second time after being overthrown
1734	Muscogee Nation chief Tomochichi from Georgia, United States, begins a six-month visit to Great Britain
1751	Pennsylvania Hospital, the first hospital in the United States, admits its first patient
1783	The American Revolutionary War officially ends with the signing of the Treaty of Paris
1873	British ocean liner the SS *Atlantic* sinks off the coast of Nova Scotia, Canada, killing 547 people
1925	Fascist dictator Adolf Hitler publishes *Mein Kampf* (*My Struggle*), outlining his antisemitism and his racist plans for Germany
2004	The US and European *Cassini-Huygens* probe takes the first close-up photos of Saturn's rings
2010	An earthquake and tsunami strike the coast of Sumatra, Indonesia, killing more than 400 people

Bibliography

*Books for young readers

Cosgrove, James A., and Neil McDaniel. *Super Suckers: The Giant Octopus and Other Cephalopods of the Pacific Coast*. Pender Harbour: Harbour Publishing, 2009.

Ellis, Richard. *Monsters of the Sea*. New York: Alfred A. Knopf, 1994.

Ellis, Richard. *The Search for the Giant Squid: The Biology and Mythology of the World's Most Elusive Creature*. New York: Penguin, 1999.

Hanlon, Roger T., and John B. Messenger. *Cephalopod Behaviour*. Cambridge: Cambridge University Press, 2018.

Heuvelmans, Bernard. *In the Wake of the Sea-Serpents*. New York: Hill and Wang, 1968.

Hoyt, Erich. *Creatures of the Deep: In Search of the Sea's Monsters and the World They Live In*. Richmond Hill: Firefly Books, 2021.

*Newquist, H. P. *Here There Be Monsters: The Legendary Kraken and the Giant Squid*. New York: Houghton Mifflin, 2010.

Nouvian, Claire. *The Deep: The Extraordinary Creatures of the Abyss*. Chicago: The University of Chicago Press, 2007.

Williams, Wendy. *Kraken: The Curious, Exciting, and Slightly Disturbing Science of Squid*. New York: Abrams Press, 2022.